Aboriginal Global Pioneers
Book 1

Australian Aboriginal Origins

Earliest Beginnings

Marji Hill

Published by The Prison Tree Press 2024
Copyright © 2024 Marji Hill

The Prison Tree Press
Suite 124
1-10 Albert Avenue
Broadbeach, Queensland 4218
https://marjihill.com
https://www.fastselfpublishing.com

Disclaimer:
All the material contained in this book is provided for educational and informational purposes only. No responsibility can be taken for any results or outcomes resulting from the use of this material.

While every care has been taken to trace and acknowledge copyright the publishers tender their apologies for any accidental infringement where copyright has proved untraceable.

Every attempt has been made to provide information that is both accurate and effective, however, the author does not assume any responsibility for the accuracy or use/misuse of this information.

Acknowledgement is given to Canva for most of the illustrations in this book.

A catalogue record for this work is available from the National Library of Australia

Aboriginal Global Pioneers (Series of 5 Books)

Australian Aboriginal Origins: Earliest Beginnings (Book 1)
Australian Aboriginal Trade: Sharing Goods and Services (Book 2
Australian Aboriginal Religion: Country and Dreaming (Book 3)
Australian Aboriginal Fire: Managing Country (Book 4)
Australian Aboriginal Medicine: Caring for People (Book 5)

ISBN 978-0-9756571-2-6 Hardback
ISBN 978-0-9756571-3-3 eBook

Australian Non-Fiction | First Nations | History

Acknowledgements

I acknowledge the Traditional Custodians of Country
throughout Australia
and their connections to land, sea, and community.

I pay my respect to elders, past, present, and emerging
and extend my respect to all First Nations peoples today.

In the spirit of reconciliation,
my mission is to increase understanding
between the First Nations and other Australians
and to provide people from all over the globe
some basic understanding of Australia's first people,
their history, and cultures.

Marji Hill

Contents

GLOBAL PIONEERS

Australia is the earliest centre of civilisation in the world that continues into the present day.

The original inhabitants of the Australian continent were First Nations people. For at least 65,000 years they occupied mainland Australia, well before modern human settlement of Europe and the Americas.

Australia's first people were global pioneers in many ways.

Sea voyagers

They were among the first great sea voyagers.

When the sea levels were much lower than they are today, much of what is now Southeast Asia was connected by land.

Between 40,000 and 100,000 years ago, First Nations people had to cross the waters between what is now known as northern Australia and the islands of Southeast Asia.

Technology

First Nations people developed sophisticated technologies.

They developed complex techniques for creating stone tools and weapons, showcasing their deep understanding and remarkable skill. They crafted a variety of tools from materials available from their natural surroundings.

Aerodynamics

The boomerang is one of the most well-known symbols of Australian First Nations culture. Its unique design not only captures the imagination but also demonstrates an early understanding of aerodynamics.

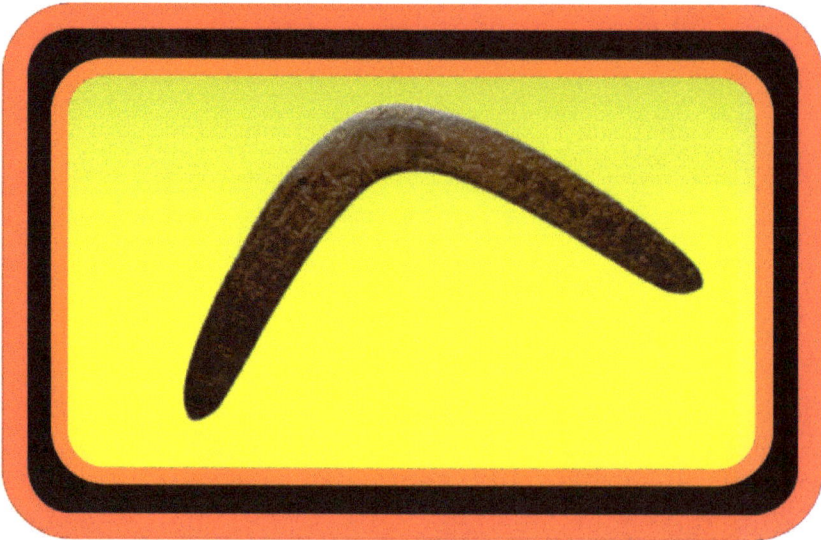

Boomerang

When thrown correctly, this ancient tool demonstrates the ingenuity and resourcefulness of First Nations people as they created a device that could return to its thrower.

This remarkable feature is achieved through careful shaping and throwing techniques, which manipulate air currents to create lift and drag, causing the boomerang to loop back.

The boomerang is a link to the long presence of First Nations people on this continent.

It features in creation stories.

The earliest dating for boomerangs in Australia is found in the peat bog at Wyrie Swamp in South Australia. Boomerangs found there have been dated as more than 10,000 years old.

But images of boomerangs can be found on rock paintings in northern Australia and are believed to be around 20,000 years old.

Land conservation and management

First Nations Australians understood the dynamics of land conservation and management. They didn't just live in one type of environment. They adapted to living in dry deserts, lush rainforests, and everything in between.

Each environment required its own special knowledge of how to find food, water, and shelter. For example, in desert areas where water is scarce, they learned to find hidden sources of water and knew when certain plants would provide nourishment.

In cooler rainforest regions, they had to understand the seasons and animal behaviours to successfully hunt and gather food resources.

First Nations people were extremely knowledgeable about their environment.

This meant knowing when to move to new areas, what animals were available to hunt, and which plants were safe to eat. Their deep understanding of the land allowed them to navigate and thrive.

Fire was used to manage the land, encourage plant growth, and drive game animals into specific areas for easier hunting. This practice also helped reduce the risk of uncontrolled bushfires by removing dry underbrush.

Fire was used to manage the land

The use of fire in such strategic ways highlights their deep ecological knowledge and sophisticated land management techniques.

Religion

First Nations people developed a religious, social and cultural life that recognised the essential link between mankind and the land.

Burial rituals from 40,000 years ago demonstrated that First Nations people had religious beliefs. The early ritual expression evidenced at Lake Mungo in southwestern New South Wales revealed they had a firmly held belief in spiritual matters.

Once again this points to their being global pioneers and part of the world's oldest continuing civilisation.

Art

First Nations people demonstrated their ability to reach for the stars in art, in legend and oral history.

They painted images on rock 30,000 years ago and possibly even as far back as 65,000 years. This means that Australia is home to some of the world's earliest rock art.

Australia is home to some of the world's earliest rock art

Not only that but artists are still creating art on rock today. In the Kimberleys in Western Australia rock art is mostly painted with different kinds of ochre.

Ochre, a natural clay earth pigment in different colours, works well with sandstone and has the capacity to last thousands of years.

Ochre was traditionally obtained from specific sites considered sacred. Its application in art and ritual shows its importance within First Nations societies.

The artists used these pigments to decorate caves, rocks, and even bodies during special ceremonies, playing a crucial role in storytelling and maintaining cultural heritage.

Ochre tells us a lot about history. The evidence of ochre means it was being used not only for making art but also in religious ritual.

Ochre

So, what was happening in the context of art making and religion over 40,000 years ago still happens today.

Medicine

First Nations people were also global pioneers in medicine. Their healing practices were not just about treating physical ailments.

They also involved understanding the spiritual and emotional well-being of individuals. They drew on ancient religious and spiritual beliefs in combination with natural remedies drawn from their intimate knowledge of natural substances like bush medicines.

These ancient healing practices have been passed down through generations, giving us a rich history of bush medicines and spiritual insights that continue to be relevant today.

FIRST NATIONS PEOPLE TODAY

According to the 2021 Census, the First Nations population in Australia was 812,728 representing 3.2 per cent of the Australian population.

In 1788 the First Nations population was estimated to be somewhere between five hundred thousand and a million inhabitants. However, some researchers say the numbers could have been as few as three hundred thousand people and as many as three million.

Today, First Nations people live throughout Australia in every state and territory. While many live in towns and cities others live in remote communities particularly in North Queensland, Northern Territory, Western Australia and South Australia.

Two groups

First Nations Australians are made up of two separate groups - Aboriginal Australians and Torres Strait Islanders.

The High Court of Australia in 1983 defined Aboriginal and Torres Strait Islander identity. The Court established three criteria to identify an Aboriginal or Torres Strait Islander person…

a person of Aboriginal or Torres Strait Islander descent;

who identifies as an Aboriginal or Torres Strait Islander;
and,

is accepted as such by the community in which he or she
lives.

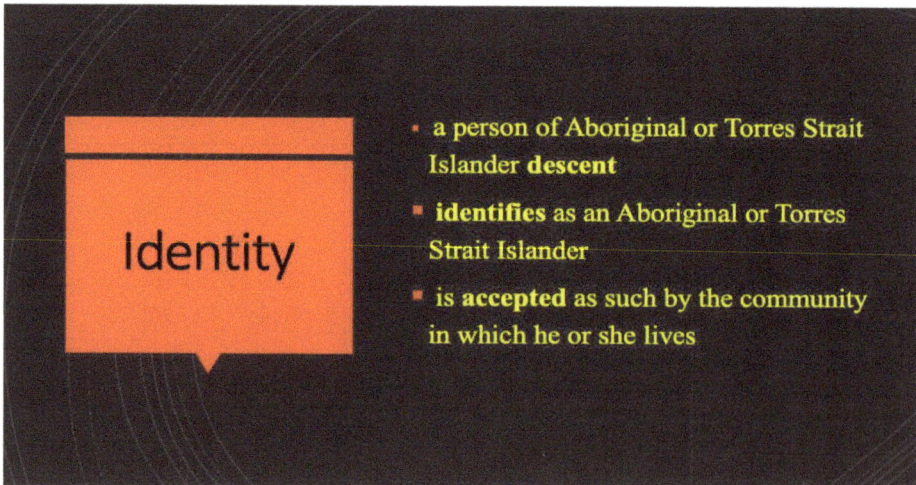

There are different ways of describing First Nations
Australians.

The usage of "Aboriginal and Torres Strait Islander" is an
acceptable practice. Other terms such as "First Nations" or
"First Peoples" are also acceptable.

This terminology recognises the variety and diversity of
Aboriginal and Torres Strait Islander cultures and their
identities in Australia.

For the purpose of this series of books, the term First Nations
people is used.

Prior to 1788, the original Australians did not use the word
"Aborigines". First Nations people used their own names — that
were local to their people. Historically and today, First Nations

people are made up of many diverse groups with many cultures and languages.

In Australia there were over 250 separate and distinct cultural and language groups speaking around 700 dialects. They continue to use the names and language applicable to their own group.

It was the British colonisers who gave the name "Aborigine" to the original inhabitants.

While the term Aboriginal or Aborigine applies to First Nations Australians, most Aboriginal people prefer to be called by their own group or regional name.

Examples are:

> Wiradjuri,
> Gurindji,
> Pitjantjatjara,
> Larrakia.

Likewise, Torres Strait Islanders prefer to be known by their island names such as Saibai Islander.

First Nations people themselves will use terms like Koori, Murri or Nunga to refer to their people or will use terms like the "saltwater people" or "spinifex people".

Torres Strait Islanders

The Torres Strait is that body of water that lies between Australia and Papua New Guinea. It was named after the Spanish navigator, Luis Vaez de Torres who sailed into the Strait in 1606.

The people living on the islands in the Strait are called the Torres Strait Islanders.

Torres Strait Island flag

Four sets of islands make up the Torres Strait:

> the western islands,
>> including Badu, Mabuiag, Thursday Island (Waiben), Moa and Muralag;

> the central islands,
>> including Yam;

> the northern islands,
>> including Saibai; and,

> the eastern islands,
>> including Darnley Island (Erub) and Mer.

Today, many Torres Strait Islanders live on the Australian mainland.

ORIGINS

Many First Nations people believe that their origins lay in Australia — that human beings were created in this vast continent.

They believe that people have always been in Australia ever since the land was created.

This is Dreamtime belief.

The Dreamtime is the religion of Australia's first people. All of life and culture started in the Dreamtime.

The Dreamtime

The Dreamtime was that timeless world when all-powerful beings rose up from a dark world and moved over a featureless earth. It was that creative time when the great Ancestral beings journeyed across the continent and had their adventures.

They created the universe, the land, the animals, plants and all geographical features. Ancestral beings roamed the country carving out the valleys, the rivers, and the mountains.

During their adventures they left behind the caverns, the rocks, the shady pools with their own spirit children. They left all living things and laid the moral and physical foundations for human society.

Dreamtime stories tell about the creative exploits of the Ancestral beings.

These creative Ancestral beings continue to carry out their creative work by renewing all of life in the land.

Where did First Nations people come from?

Did First Nations people originate in Australia or did they come from somewhere else?

Scientific evidence is limited and there is a lot of debate.

Research by archaeologists unveils the story of Australia's first people.

Scientific evidence suggests dates for human occupation may go as far back as 100,000 years.

At least it seems that First Nations people have a continuous history dating back 65,000 years.

Scientists have observed many similarities between the hunter-gatherer lifestyle of people in Australia with that in Asia.

Because of these similarities scientists argue that the first Australians must have migrated from Southeast Asia.

Sea crossing

There could have been a lot of migrations.

The question is:

> was the migration of people to Australia deliberate,
>   or,
> was the migration or migrations accidental?

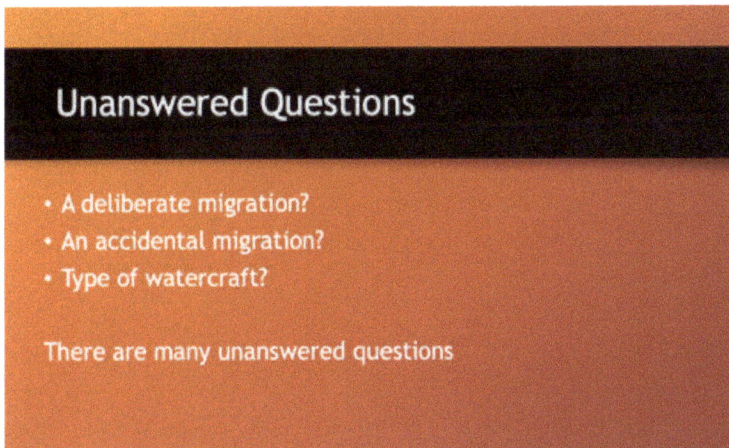

Unanswered Questions

• A deliberate migration?
• An accidental migration?
• Type of watercraft?

There are many unanswered questions

The first Australians probably came when the sea levels were low and when it was only a very short journey to travel over water from Asia to Australia.

When the tide levels were low Australia, New Guinea and Tasmania were joined to form the one continent.

If they came by water the original Australians must have developed suitable watercraft to make the journey by sea.

The general consensus among prehistorians is that the first Australians came to the southern continent via Southeast Asia.

It does seem certain that there was some kind of major sea crossing.

The question is whether this crossing was something deliberate or whether it was an accidental crossing.

If the migration was accidental, First Nations Australians could have been caught in monsoonal winds and drifted across to the continent.

As the first sea voyagers they would have had to travel over water of less than 100 kilometres (approximately 62 miles).

What kind of boat or watercraft did they arrive in?

We do not even know what kind of boat or watercraft they came in. There are no remains of boats for the scientists to examine.

It is hard for archaeologists to determine the kind of water transport the people came in.

Could they have come by some kind of boat or raft?

There are many unanswered questions.

Climate change

Going back 100,000 years or more, a lot of changes took place to the climate and the environment of Australia.

Over time the continent experienced dramatic environmental change.

The drowning of the land between Australia and Papua New Guinea marked the gradual ending of the Ice Age which lasted from about 80,000 to 7,000 years ago.

Great areas of land that are now under the sea were once the homelands of First Nations people.

When the sea levels were low the Australian landmass included Papua New Guinea and Tasmania.

The Torres Strait was a deep valley with several high mountains which today form some of the Western Islands in Torres Strait.

Over time environmental change was dramatic.

Consequently, the condition of the land was very different to that of today.

There were once volcanoes in many parts of the country and activity sculptured the landscape.

A massive volcano in the Tweed region of northern New South Wales, for example, was active some 23 million years ago. Then about 10 million years ago it began to die.

In the process the magnificent, classic erosion caldera landform of Wollumbin (commonly known as Mount Warning) was created. This deeply sacred mountain was the volcano's epicentre.

Wollumbin (Mt Warning)

Parts of the continent such as the Willandra Lakes area in southwest New South Wales which are now very dry were well watered and with lots of people living there.

The area was once a flourishing centre of life. The inhabitants lived on the birds and fish from the lakes.

There was plenty of plant life and animals for food resources.

Megafauna

There were dinosaurs.

Giant marsupials roamed the country. There was the giant wombat (*diprotodon*), the giant kangaroo (*procoptodon*) and the leopard-sized meat eating marsupial lion (*thylacoleo*).

Giant kangaroos could eat the leaves growing on trees three metres from the ground.

There were dinosaurs

The whole of the country was wetter and hotter than our current climate and there was abundant vegetation that is not here today.

These animals moved over the land, enjoying the lush tropical jungles and flora.

The question is whether the peopling of the continent wiped out the megafauna; scientists think they probably lived side by side for a very long time.

At the end of the last ice age, Australia's climate changed. What was once cold and dry became warm and dry and inland water became scarce.

Lakes became dry.

The large animals lost their habitat. They retreated to a narrow band in eastern Australia, where there was permanent water and better vegetation.

The first people that lived in those ancient times developed social organisations, developed, adapted and refined technology, managed the land, controlled plant growth and had highly developed complex religious beliefs.

The success of the First Nations people speaks much of their abilities as also demonstrated by their art, jewellery and adornment, advanced tool technology, watercraft construction and religious burial rites.

LAKE MUNGO

Archaeologists gathered scientific evidence from Lake Mungo that showed First Nations people were living in south-eastern Australia 40,000 years ago.

This is one of several dry lakes in the World Heritage listed Willandra Lakes Region in south-western New South Wales. What was once a rich and thriving environment flourishing with life and vegetation eventually became barren, arid and desert-like.

Mungo Lady

Human remains were found at Lake Mungo. These were carbon-dated as being from 40,000 to 42,000 years ago.

In 1968 archaeologists found human bones which they named Mungo Lady.

Archaeologist

They concluded that these remains had been ritually buried. Red ochre which was found on the remains was the evidence that there had been some form of religious ritual practised in those ancient times.

Mungo Lady had been cremated, her bones crushed, burned again and buried in a mound of sand. They are the oldest remains ever found in Australia.

Mungo Man

Some years later another skeleton was found at Lake Mungo. This time it was a male corpse. He was given the name Mungo Man and he lived there all those years ago.

Mungo Man was around 50 years old. Like Mungo Lady, he had been buried in a religious ritual. He had been placed on his back, his hands crossed his lap, and his body was sprinkled with red ochre.

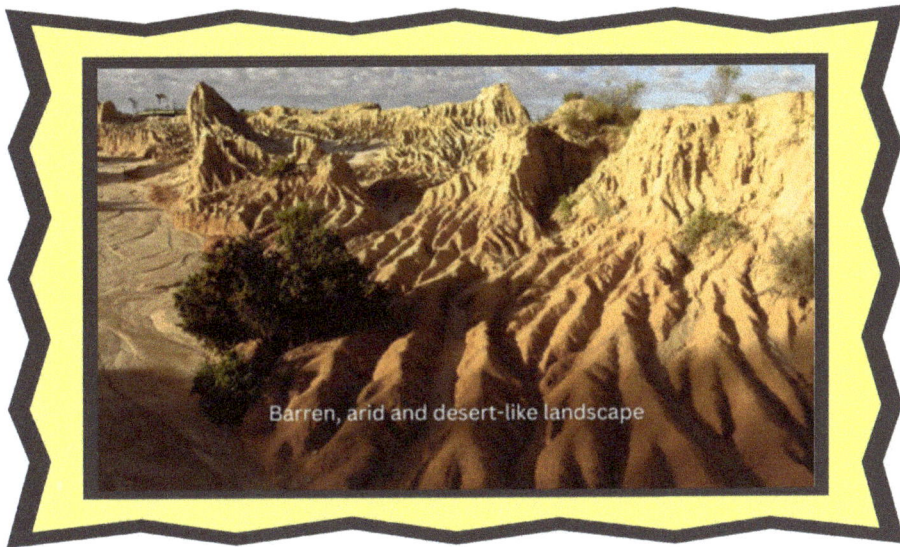

Barren, arid and desert-like landscape

Lake Mungo Willandra Lakes Region

Given that pigments such as ochre tell us a lot about the past, the evidence is clear that ochre was used in art and in religious rituals in those ancient times and is still used today.

The Lake Mungo site, where the remains of Mungo Man and Mungo Lady were discovered, show that Australia's first people had complex religious beliefs.

The positioning of the bodies and the use of red ochre in the burials indicate rituals and traditions that included honouring the deceased and possibly an understanding of an afterlife.

There was a holistic belief system deeply embedded in their culture, reinforcing connections between their daily lives and spiritual world.

ANCIENT ROCK SHELTER

Prehistorians and archaeologists have sophisticated dating techniques which help us get a more accurate understanding of the origins of how people came to be in Australia.

Archaeological site

Some of the earliest archaeological sites are found in northern Australia.

There is a very important sandstone rock shelter in the Northern Territory. This is Madjedbebe. It was formerly known as Malakunanja II.

It is situated on the western side of Arnhem Land approximately 40 kilometres (25 miles) west of the East Alligator River.

This ancient rock shelter is Australia's oldest documented site of human habitation.

Archaeological evidence from excavations from here tells us that human beings may have been living in this area for more than 55,000 years ago, probably 65,000 years if not more.

Ancient grinding stones, stone axes and ochre point to the earliest known evidence for seed grinding and intensive plant use.

In addition, the evidence of ochre and motifs on the rock walls indicates a possible tradition of artistic endeavour all those years ago.

Generations have continued to link past traditions with contemporary First Nations life. First Nations artists still draw inspiration from ancient techniques and themes, creating modern works that reflect a rich cultural heritage.

The incorporation of traditional symbols and stories in art, blend the old and the new. This fusion not only preserves ancient traditions but also allows contemporary cultures to evolve and adapt to a changing world.

IN SUMMARY

In this book we have explored the incredible history and achievements of First Nations people as global pioneers who have lived continuously in Australia for more than 65,000 years.

These early Australians understood their environments deeply, using plants, animals, and even controlled fire to sustain their way of life. They have been and continue to be a resilient and innovative people whose traditions continue to enrich Australia's cultural heritage today.

First Nations cultures are the oldest living cultures in the world. Australia's earliest people developed a social and cultural life, developed technology, managed the land, controlled plant growth, and had a highly developed religious set of beliefs.

They demonstrated their ability to reach for the stars in art, in legend and oral history.

Glossary

Archaeologist A person who studies human history and prehistory through the excavation of sites and the analysis of artefacts and other physical remains.

Pigment A powdered substance when mixed with a liquid gives colour to other materials.

Prehistorian An archaeologist who specialises in prehistory

Sandstone A sedimentary rock consisting mainly of fragments of sand

Technology The application of scientific knowledge for practical purposes or applications

Sources

The author acknowledges the following sources of information.

Australian InFo International 1989 *Australian Aboriginal Culture.* Canberra, AGPS Press.

Hill, Marji 2021 *First People Then and Now: Introducing Indigenous Australians.* 2nd ed. Broadbeach, Qld, The Prison Tree Press.

Who is Marji Hill

Marji Hill, artist and painter since childhood, runs her art career alongside her career as an author.

She is a highly respected international author as well as a seasoned business executive, researcher and coach.

Marji is passionate about promoting understanding between Australia's first people and other Australians.

The spirit of reconciliation was fostered in all her writings ever since she was a Research Fellow in Education at the Australian Institute of Aboriginal and Torres Strait Islander Studies (AIATSIS) in Canberra.

From 2008 to 2011, Marji was Deputy Chairperson of the Mosman Branch of Reconciliation Australia in Sydney.

Following her Research Fellowship at AIATSIS in 1976 Marji, together with her late partner, Alex Barlow, produced more than seventy (70) books on all aspects of the First Nations people including the critical, annotated bibliography *Black Australia*.

In 1989 she was the Project Coordinator and one of the researchers and writers of *Australian Aboriginal Culture* the official Australian Government publication on First Nations people.

In 1988 *Six Australian Battlefields* was published by Angus and Robertson. A decade later it was re-published by Allen & Unwin as a paperback edition.

Her nine-volume encyclopaedia, *Macmillan Encyclopaedia of Australia's Aboriginal Peoples* was published in 2000 and in 2009 she published *The Apology: Saying Sorry To The Stolen Generations.*

Marji's more recent publications extend to self-improvement and self-help with books like *Staying Young Growing Old* and *Inspired by Country* a self-help book about painting with gouache.

More Books by Marji Hill

First Nations

Hill, Marji 2021 *Australian Aboriginal History: 5 Stories of Indigenous Heroes.* Broadbeach, Qld, The Prison Tree Press.

Hill, Marji 2021 *First People Then and Now: Introducing Indigenous Australians.* 2nd ed. Broadbeach, Qld, The Prison Tree Press.

Aboriginal Global Pioneers

Hill, Marji 2024 *Australian Aboriginal Origins: Earliest Beginnings.* Broadbeach, Qld, The Prison Tree Press. (Book 1)

Hill, Marji 2024 *Australian Aboriginal Trade: Sharing Goods and Services.* Broadbeach, Qld, The Prison Tree Press. (Book 2)

Hill, Marji 2024 *Australian Aboriginal Religion: Country and Dreaming.* Broadbeach, Qld, The Prison Tree Press. (Book 3)

Hill, Marji 2024 *Australian Aboriginal Fire: Managing Country.* Broadbeach, Qld, The Prison Tree Press. (Book 4)

Hill, Marji 2024 *Australian Aboriginal Medicine: Caring for People.* Broadbeach, Qld, The Prison Tree Press. (Book 5)

Self-improvement/Self-Help

Hill, Marji 2014 *Staying Young Growing Old.* Broadbeach, Qld, The Prison Tree Press.

Hill, Marji 2020 *How Big Is Your Why? An Author's Guide to Time Management and Productivity to Achieve Transformational Results.* Broadbeach, Qld, The Prison Tree Press.

Hill, Marji 2020 *A Create and Publish Toolbox: 101 Prompts In A Guided Journal To Help You Write, Self-publish, And Market Your Book On Amazon.* Broadbeach, Qld, The Prison Tree Press.

Hill, Marji 2021 *Inspired by Country: An Artist's Journey Back to Nature, Landscape Painting with Gouache.* Broadbeach, Qld, The Prison Tree Press.

Hill, Marji 2024 *Australian Paintings: Artworks by Marji Hill.* Broadbeach, Qld, The Prison Tree Press.

Gold

Hill, Marji 2022 *Gates of Gold: The Discovery of Gold, its Legacy and its Contribution to Australian Identity* Broadbeach, Qld, The Prison Tree Press.

Hill, Marji 2022 *Shadows of Gold: Eureka and the Birth of Australian Democracy.* Broadbeach, Qld, The Prison Tree Press.

Hill, Marji 2022 *Gold and the Chinese: Racism, Riots and Protest on the Australian Goldfields.* Broadbeach, Qld, The Prison Tree Press.

Hill, Marji 2022 *Ghosts of Gold: The Life and Times of Jupiter Mosman.* Broadbeach, Qld, The Prison Tree Press.

Hill, Marji 2022 *Blood Gold: Native Police, Bushrangers & Law and Order on the Goldfields.* Broadbeach, Qld, The Prison Tree Press.

www.ingramcontent.com/pod-product-compliance
Lightning Source LLC
Chambersburg PA
CBHW040254100426
42811CB00011B/1261